JAMES PATTERSON

ALL ABOUT THE AUTHOR™

JAMES PATTERSON

SUSAN NICHOLS

ROSEN
PUBLISHING®

New York

Published in 2016 by The Rosen Publishing Group, Inc.
29 East 21st Street, New York, NY 10010

Copyright © 2016 by The Rosen Publishing Group, Inc.

First Edition

Library of Congress Cataloging-in-Publication Data

Nichols, Susan, 1975-
James Patterson / Susan Nichols. -- First edition.
    pages cm. -- (All about the author)
Includes bibliographical references and index.
ISBN 978-1-4994-6274-6 (library bound)
1. Patterson, James, 1947--Juvenile literature. 2. Authors, American--20th century--Biography--Juvenile literature. I. Title.
PS3566.A822Z8 2016
813'.54--dc23
[B]
                                                    2015020297

Manufactured in China

CONTENTS

James Patterson, one of the English language's best-selling novelists, had a problem.

Patterson was regularly publishing several novels a year. In fact, he was producing so many books that he eventually had to hire other writers to help him draft his manuscripts. His books were being turned into movies starring major celebrities, like Morgan Freeman, Ashley Judd, and Monica Potter. Other books were being discussed by producers who wanted to turn them into prime-time television programs. Anyone who entered a U.S. bookstore could find dozens of his books on the shelves. In England, he was the most borrowed author from the British library system. In any library, the "P" section in fiction was especially hefty because several shelves were filled with Patterson's novels.

So what was the problem? Despite the fact that millions of readers around the world loved his novels, he had a son who disliked

James Brendan Patterson is one of the most widely read authors in the world. Over the course of his career, he has sold more than 300 million books.

books. It is a writer's worst nightmare to have a child who dislikes the very thing that inspires that writer every day: a love of reading.

This was quite disturbing because James Patterson knew how vital reading would be to his son's future. He was aware of how many studies demonstrated that poor reading skills could inter-fere with schoolwork and, later, with finding a good job. He also knew that the brain is like a muscle: the more you use it, the stronger it becomes. In other words, the more you read, the better you become at reading.

Patterson and his wife, Susan, decided that it was not the job of Jack's teachers to make sure their son liked to read—it was *their* job, as his par-ents. Sparking an interest in reading had to start in their home. And what better home to inspire a young person to read than that of the Pattersons, which was inhabited by the world's most popular author?

James and Sue decided to strike a deal with their young son. Even though the Pattersons were wealthy, they required their son to do certain chores around the home. One of those was mowing the lawn. That year, when school let out for the summer, Patterson told Jack that he did not have to do any chores that summer. However, he did have to read every single day, for a set amount of time.

Jack balked at the deal at first: he wanted to spend his summer enjoying time off from school. He didn't want to do anything that resembled school-work. However, James Patterson promised Jack something he called the "Reading Can Be a Joy" Guarantee. He explained to Jack that reading doesn't have to feel like work—it can be fun. To prove it, he helped Jack pick out several books he would enjoy, including *The Lightning Thief, A Wrinkle in Time,* and several others.

Jack reluctantly sat down every day that summer and fulfilled his promise, while his parents watched anxiously to see if they had been right: Could they light a spark and a passion for reading in their bored eight-year-old?

ONE

TOUGH BEGINNINGS

I t probably shouldn't have surprised James Patterson that his son was not interested in reading. He may have imagined, for a moment, that he was looking at his own past. The truth was that the young James Patterson himself had never really been interested in reading.

James Brendan Patterson was born in Newburgh, New York, on March 22, 1947. Newburgh is a small city located sixty miles (ninety-seven kilometers) north of New York City, along the Hudson River. Patterson was born after World War II (1939–1945) had ended, when Newburgh was experiencing a population boom. In 1950, the city's popula-tion reached a record high of 32,000 people. Today, Newburgh is considered part of the New York metropolitan area.

THE ALL-AMERICAN CITY

When Patterson was born, Newburgh was a pleasant suburb with plenty of small, local businesses and large, open areas and fields. However, after the war, new highways connected many parts of New York to one another, and a wave of big businesses moved in, which drove out smaller businesses. The city began to decline. Young people began leaving Newburgh rather than settling in their hometown.

George Washington spent several months in James Patterson's hometown of Newburgh, New York, using the Hasbrouck family farmhouse as his headquarters from April 1782 to August 1783.

The city's most popular feature, its waterfront, became rundown and dangerous. In 2011, an article in *New York* magazine called Newburgh, population 29,000, the "murder capital of New York State." Author Patrick Radden Keefe wrote, "Despite its small size and bucolic setting, Newburgh occupies one of the most dangerous four-mile stretches in the northeastern United States."

During the 1940s and 1950s, however, Newburgh was a comfortable town in which to live. Patterson told the *Guardian* that it was "the all-American city" when he was a young man.

A DISTANT FATHER

Patterson's father, Charles, was a difficult person, mostly because he had led a life that was disappointing in some ways. Charles Patterson was born to very poor parents. His father, James Patterson's grandfather, abandoned his family, and so Charles's mother was left to raise several children alone. Financially, she could not survive, and she was accepted into a government-run housing facility that took in poor families. She became the charwoman, or the cleaning woman, for the facility, doing what she had to do in order to support her children.

Charles Patterson grew up in the housing facility, known back then as a "poorhouse," and worked very hard in school. After high school, he earned a scholarship to attend Hamilton College. According to his son, he had ambitions of becoming a diplomat and a writer. Instead, however, he soon found himself having to provide for a family. In an interview with *Publishers Weekly*, James Patterson said that his father had been accepted for graduate studies at Georgetown University, but he declined that dream when he found out his wife, Isabelle Morris, was pregnant with James, their first child and only son.

Three more children followed, all daughters, and Charles Patterson resigned himself to doing any work that would pay the bills. He sold insurance. He even spent six years driving a bread truck. He knew that supporting his young family was important. However, he was disappointed that he was never able to pursue his own dreams.

James Patterson remembers that his father was distant and emotionally detached. "He never had a father around himself," Patterson told the *Guardian*, "and while you did feel there was a bond, it wasn't expressed much." Patterson and his father were never very close. Charles Patterson did not show much affection toward his only son. In an interview with *Vanity Fair*, James Patterson described how severely distant his father was: "I think the first time he ever hugged me was on his deathbed."

Newburgh enjoys a beautiful waterfront. As a child, James Patterson was free to roam around the area, from the majestic Hudson River to the stretches of wooded hills and valleys. During these adventures, his imagination began to develop.

A HAPPY CHILDHOOD

Despite the distance between him and his father, James Patterson was close to his mother and sisters growing up. His mother, Isabelle, worked very hard also to support her family of four children. Isabelle Patterson had graduated from St. Joseph's College in Emmitsburg, Maryland, after which she spent thirty years as an elementary school teacher. She was devoted to her children and her students.

As a child, Patterson enjoyed the activities most kids enjoy, but he also spent a lot of time on his own. Newburgh sits in the Hudson Valley, which has beautiful views and, in the 1950s, was still not developed land. Patterson has described how he would often go off into the woods near his home alone and spend hours roaming around. This was at a time when it was normal for children to leave the house in the morning and stay outside until dinnertime. Patterson passed the time by telling himself stories, just spinning tales in his mind. In that way, he was similar to his father, who had also dreamed of being a writer, though he had never shared his dreams with his son.

Patterson's grandparents owned a restaurant in New York. Patterson spent a lot of time in that restaurant, working and helping with the daily routines of the business. He was sociable with the customers and employees. In particular, he liked spending time with one of the cooks, an African American woman who had a family of her own. Patterson

A lot has changed since James Patterson attended St. Patrick's High School in Newburgh in the 1960s, but he still manages to connect with high school students today. Through readings and speaking engagements, Patterson shares his love of reading with young people.

A POSITIVE ATTITUDE

By watching his parents and grandparents, Patterson learned the value of hard work. When he was older, Patterson once remembered a lesson that he'd been taught by his grandfather—his mother's father—a man who worked very hard and drove a frozen food truck. As a child, Patterson would sometimes accompany his grandfather on these work trips. He recalled that, despite the long hours (they would often depart at 4:00 A.M.), his grandfather always sang in a cheerful voice, as the truck climbed up the hilly roads in New York. According to an interview in the *New York Times*, Patterson's grandfather told him, "Jim, I don't care what you do when you grow up. I don't care if you drive a truck like I do, or if you become the president. Just remember that when you go over the mountain to work in the morning, you've got to be singing." In other words, it was important to enjoy what you did for a living, rather than be unhappy in your work. It was also important to have a positive attitude.

enjoyed playing and spending time with this woman and her family.

Patterson attended St. Patrick's High School, which was run by the Christian Brothers, who valued both academics and discipline. The parish of St.

Patrick's was established in the early 1800s by Irish immigrants, but it had already begun to recognize the diversity within the Newburgh area by the time James Patterson was a student at the high school. According to the St. Patrick's parish website, by the early 1960s, the parish had begun reaching out to the Spanish-speaking community, which eventually resulted in the establishment of its Hispanic Religious Education Association. Also, by the 1970s, the number of African American parishioners had begun to increase, which led to the forming of a Black Ministry in the 1980s.

James Patterson grew up in a neighborhood that was becoming more culturally diverse, and he was very comfortable engaging with people of many different cultures and backgrounds, which would have an impact on his writing style later in his life.

TWO

BECOMING A READER

Patterson was a good student, perhaps because his mother was a schoolteacher. However, he actually did not enjoy reading very much, although he enjoyed writing sometimes. In an interview with the *Telegraph*, he described how he enjoyed the process of "scribbling," as he calls it— sketching out little stories.

However, he was more focused on getting good grades than on being creative. He felt like he had to excel in his classes. In an interview with *Vanity Fair*, he said, "I think that I felt I needed to be this very bright, first-in-his class kind of kid, for whatever reason, pretty serious." And he was—when he graduated from St. Patrick's High School, he was named valedictorian. He hoped to enroll in one of the country's best universities. He worked hard and prepared applications to Harvard, Yale, Bates, and other top-tier colleges, and then he waited anxiously for the results.

The news was both disappointing and surprising. Disappointing because he was not accepted into any of the schools to which he applied. Surprising because he had been accepted to Manhattan College, located in the Bronx, a borough of New York City. The reason why that acceptance was

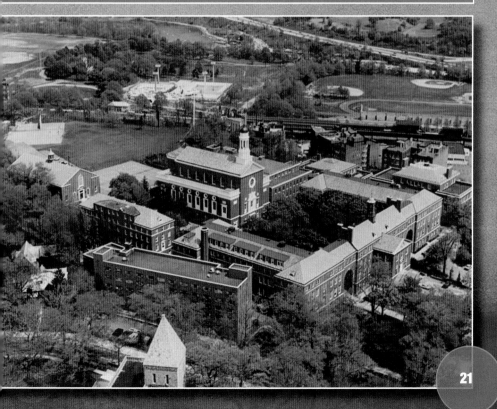

ocated in the Bronx borough of New York City, Manhattan College was a common hoice for Catholic students bound for college. James Patterson hadn't intended to attend Manhattan College, but someone had other plans for him.

surprising was that he hadn't even applied to Manhattan College.

The mystery quickly unraveled. Patterson learned that the Christian Brothers had never actually mailed off his applications to the Ivy League universities. Instead, they had applied to Manhattan College on his behalf because they had been able to secure a scholarship for him to attend. In an interview published in the *Guardian*, Patterson explained that, looking back, he was not angry at what happened. Manhattan College, he explained, was run by the Christian Brothers, and, "In those days, if you were Catholic, you went to a Catholic college."

READING THE GREATS ON THE GRAVEYARD SHIFT

By that point, Patterson's family had moved to a suburb of Boston, Massachusetts. Patterson spent the summer before he attended college with his family in Boston. To earn extra money that summer,

Patterson took a job working the night shift at McLean Hospital. Founded in 1811, the institution has housed many famous patients, including Ray Charles, James Taylor, Sylvia Plath, and Robert Lowell.

he took a job working the night shift as an aide at McLean Hospital in Belmont, Massachusetts.

Working the night shift meant being paid overtime, so Patterson was happy with the salary. However, he was not thrilled about the long, boring hours he had to spend being awake. There was a benefit to working the night shift: all those long, quiet hours meant that he could do something else with his time. Patterson decided to spend his time productively: he read books, lots of books—about ten books a week. These months spent reading

FAMOUS PATIENTS AT MCLEAN

McLean is a psychiatric institution that cares for people with mental disorders. It boasts of some famous patients, including poets Robert Lowell and Sylvia Plath, musicians Ray Charles and James Taylor, mathematician John Nash, and novelist David Foster Wallace. Patterson, who was still a teenager when he worked there, described McLean in an interview with the *Guardian*: "There was a tradition of wonderful craziness."

so much changed his perception about fiction. He became a fan of some of the most renowned writers in literary history, such as Irish novelist James Joyce, Colombian writer Gabriel Garcia Marquez, and French novelist Jean Genet.

Patterson began "scribbling" even more, trying his hand at literary fiction. More than anything, however, he continued to read; he spent the free time he had during his evenings at McLean drinking coffee and turning pages.

GRADUATE DEGREE

Patterson graduated from Manhattan College in 1969, and he had done so well that Vanderbilt University offered him a full scholarship to study English literature. He attended for one year. Vanderbilt is in Tennessee, and so he got to spend time in the American South. However, he quickly realized that studying English literature—and teaching it to future college students—was not a career for him. In an interview with the *New York Times*, Patterson said, "I had found two things I loved, reading and writing. If I became a college professor, I knew I was going to wind up killing them both off." So he dropped out of the PhD program in English and out of Vanderbilt University,

After graduating from Manhattan College, Patterson received acceptance to Vanderbilt University in Nashville, Tennessee. He planned to pursue a PhD in English Literature, but after one year, he left to go back to New York.

and he began looking for a job.

Like his father, Patterson had dropped out of a graduate program. However, there was a difference. The difference was that for James, dropping out was his own choice. Patterson had re-examined his goals in life, and he had decided that being a student for six or eight more years was not one of his aspirations.

During those weeks he spent reading in the late hours at McLean Hospital, Patterson had experienced a revelation that would become important to him later in his life. It was this: the reason he had never really enjoyed reading as a kid was not because he didn't like books. It was because he'd never been exposed to good writing by true masters like Marquez, Joyce, and Genet. A good book, he learned, can absorb a reader and keep him intrigued, keep him fascinated.

After all, nobody can resist a good story.

Patterson had decided that he did not want to spend his life studying good books—he wanted to write some of his own.

AD MAN

P atterson moved back to New York in 1971 and accepted a job as a copywriter for J. Walter Thompson, an advertising agency. Advertising is a creative industry. Advertisers have to invent songs, commercials, and other forms of media that will grab a consumer's attention and convince him or her to buy the product or service being sold. In an interview with the *Guardian,* Patterson insisted that he was never really excited about advertising. It was just a job to him. "I never particularly liked advertising and it hadn't been anything in my mind," he said.

However, as it turned out, James Patterson was exceptionally good at it. This might not surprise some people, as there are many American writers who made

careers in advertising. One was Theodor Geisel, known as Dr. Seuss, who drew ad pictures, and novelist F. Scott Fitzgerald, the author of *The Great Gatsby*. Like them, Patterson quickly gained a reputation for knowing what consumers wanted and for being creative and direct.

At this point in his life, a tragedy occurred. Patterson's longtime girlfriend died of a brain tumor. She was only in her thirties. Patterson was devastated to see how the brain tumor killed her over the course of two years. The stress and grief from her illness and death caused him to develop his own health problems. His blood pressure rose to high levels. He also developed a condition known as Bell's palsy, in which part of one's face becomes paralyzed.

To cope with his grief, Patterson dedicated himself—with even more intensity than before—to his work. He put in long hours at the office. Eventually, Patterson was named CEO of the North American division of J. Walter Thompson, overseeing one thousand employees.

Altogether, Patterson was responsible for producing hundreds of television commercials. He developed good team-working habits. Producing a commercial, for example, requires the work and contribution of many staff members. Patterson enjoyed the energy that came with working with other like-minded people. He found that creativity is contagious when one is working with the right set of people.

FAMOUS ADS BY JAMES PATTERSON

While working for the J. Walter Thompson agency, James Patterson handled accounts for major clients, including Burger King and Kodak. One of his clients was the Ford Motor Company, for which he wrote the famous slogan, "Have you driven a Ford lately?" And every child who grew up in the 1980s and 1990s knows the slogan he wrote for another client, the Toys "R" Us company. The well-known jingle? "I don't wanna grow up. I'm a Toys 'R' Us kid."

DISCOVERING COMMERCIAL FICTION

He also discovered something else he enjoyed. In addition to reading great, classic literature, he discovered commercial fiction, or "genre fiction," as it is sometimes called. Commercial fiction is a label for novels that appeal to a wide audience; some people who criticize commercial fiction say it appeals to so many people because the language is not very sophisticated or complicated. (Two very recent best sellers that were works of commercial fiction were *The Hunger Games,* by Suzanne Collins, and the *Twilight* series by Stephanie Meyer. These novels were enjoyed by teenagers as well as adults.) Commercial fiction is based more on plot—that is, on the sequence of actions—than on other elements of literature, such as character, theme, and writing style. One mark of commercial fiction is that it can easily fall into a fictional category, or genre, such as "mystery," "romance," "science fiction," or "fantasy."

While working at the J. Walter Thompson agency, Patterson read a best-selling work of commercial fiction: *The Exorcist*, by William Peter Blatty. The novel tells the story of a young girl with a mysterious, terrifying illness. Desperate for answers, her mother consults doctors but gets no help. Finally, she consults the Catholic Church, which concludes that the girl has been

Patterson was taken by the 1971 novel *The Exorcist*, which was adapted by the book's author into a major motion picture. *The Exorcist* became one of the most popular horror movies of all time, and its success inspired James Patterson.

possessed by the devil. The church officials send an "exorcist," an expert at purging the devil from people, to rid the girl of the satanic spirits within her. The novel had gone on to become a major motion picture, and it is still considered one of the best horror films of all time. The screenplay for the film was also written by the book's author, a point that would be important to Patterson when his own books were adapted to film.

Patterson read *The Exorcist*, and he thought that he could write something like that. As a teenager, he had "scribbled." Now, he began writing seriously. Patterson purchased a typewriter and set it up on the kitchen table of his apartment. He spent his evenings, as well as weekends, working at that typewriter. Often, he spent his lunch breaks at the office working on drafts of his stories as well.

A PUBLISHED NOVELIST

Finally, he produced a novel that made him proud. It was titled *The Thomas Berryman Number*, and it was a murder mystery set in Nashville, Tennessee, where Patterson had lived for a year while attending Vanderbilt University. In the novel, a newspaper reporter investigates the assassination of the mayor of Nashville. He realizes that there is an assassin, named Thomas Berryman, who is an expert at making murder look like an accident.

Excited, Patterson followed the usual route to get a book published—he got an agent, who tried to sell the book on Patterson's behalf by sending it to several publishers. It was rejected thirty-one times.

Patterson tried to stay hopeful. Eventually, he was contacted by Little, Brown and Company. The publisher, based in New York City, decided to publish the novel and pay Patterson $8,500, according to Jonathan Mahler in a *New York Times* article. Patterson was happy; *The Thomas Berryman Number* was published in 1976 and sold ten thousand copies, which was not bad for a first-time author. The critical reviews of the book were also good. The *Los Angeles Times* called the book "compelling" and "chilling," and the *Houston Chronicle* described the chapters as "bursting with surprise and suspense." Finally, James Patterson could officially say that he was a writer.

The administrators of the Edgar Award, an annual prize given to mystery writers, called him one day and asked if he was attending that year's ceremony. Patterson said he was not sure, and the caller eventually spilled a secret: Patterson had been named as winner of the award for best first novel. They urged him to attend the ceremony

Grand Master 2010
Dorothy Gilman

The Edgar Award is the most prestigious award in the genre of mystery writing. It is appropriately named after Edgar Allan Poe, who is credited with inventing the mystery story in American writing.

and accept his award, and Patterson did. "So I went," he said in an interview with the *Guardian*. "[I] sweated until they said my name. And when I had my little moment to say something I said, 'I guess I'm a writer now.'"

Patterson continued working long hours at J. Walter Thompson, however, because writing novels did not pay his bills. Furthermore, his second novel, *Season of the Machete* (1977), was a disappointment to booksellers and also to Patterson himself. Many people liked it, but many did not.

And then, in 1993, Patterson got an idea for a new book, and a new character: Alex Cross.

FOUR

FULL-TIME WRITER

In 1993, Patterson wrote *Along Came a Spider*, a mystery thriller novel that featured a character whom readers immediately loved: Alex Cross. As Patterson imagined him, Cross is an African American police detective and psychiatrist in Washington, DC. Cross is also a single father who loves his job and his family, but he soon encounters one of his most difficult cases: a double kidnapping that has everybody on the police force stumped.

Patterson sensed that, in Alex Cross, he had created a character that would be popular. He wanted to ensure that readers would hear about *Along Came a Spider*; he wanted to sell more than ten thousand books. He wanted to sell a million.

The game is far from over

MORGAN FREEMAN
along came a spider

In 2001, a movie version of *Along Came a Spider* was released. It starred renowned actor Morgan Freeman in the role of Alex Cross, and Monica Potter as Jezzie Flannigan.

PUSHING THE PUBLISHING BOUNDARIES

He parlayed his skills as an ad man when marketing the novel. He suggested to his publisher, Little, Brown and Company, that it produce a television commercial to advertise the book. The publishers balked at this suggestion: a TV commercial to sell a book? Weren't books and television supposed to be opposites? After all, reading was an activity people did instead of watching television. It didn't feel right. After all, people watch commercials and are persuaded to buy products like breakfast cereal or household cleaners. Readers don't look to commercials to make decisions about which books to read—for that, they look to their friends, their librarians, and their teachers. Therefore, the publishers refused.

Patterson was annoyed. He knew the power of television, and he saw no conflict between television and books. He decided to make the commercial on his own. After all, who was better suited to the task than the CEO of a major advertising firm? Patterson spent $2,000 of his own money producing it. When the editors at Little, Brown and Company saw it, they immediately agreed to pay for some of the costs. They realized that the commercial could help boost book sales.

It absolutely did, to a level that surprised everyone.

The commercial ran in three major American cities: New York, Washington, DC, and Chicago, cities in which there was a large number of readers who purchased thriller novels. When *Along Came a Spider* was finally released, it debuted at number 9 on the *New York Times* best-seller list, a weekly compilation of books that are selling the most copies in American bookstores. James Patterson had been a writer, but now he was a best-selling author.

RECEPTION TO THE NOVEL

Readers loved the character of Alex Cross, and many wondered how Patterson, who is white, could create such a realistic African American character. Patterson attributed his depiction to his familiarity with African American culture, such as the cook who worked for his grandparents' restaurant. He had been close to her and her family as a child. In an interview with *Time* magazine, he explained, "I always kept them

BREAKING STEREOTYPES

In an interview, Patterson explained a major reason why he created his famous character Alex Cross as an African American. Patterson described how he had noticed the way African American characters were negatively stereotyped in literature and film. African Americans were usually typecast as criminals or other roles that were not uplifting. As a result, Patterson challenged himself to "create an African-American character who solved problems with his intelligence," as stated in an interview with Noah Charney.

in the back of my head, and the aura of that household is part of what drove me to create the Cross family. So it's not just Alex."

More books quickly followed *Along Came a Spider*. In 1996, Patterson decided to quit his full-time job as CEO of J. Walter Thompson. He simply needed more time to write books.

Over the years, he has created several mystery/thriller series, including the *Women's Murder Club* series, with characters Lindsay Boxer, Cindy Thomas, Claire Washburn, and Jill Bernhardt. Later, Yuki Castellano also joins the cast of characters. Patterson was success-ful at writing novels with female protagonists, which is a challenge for a male writer.

Patterson has a large home in Florida, where he spends most of his time. He writes every day of the week, 365 days a year, working on new novels, collaborations with cowriters, and movie scripts.

JAMES PATTERSON, THE BRAND

By this time, Patterson had so many ideas that he realized he could not write them all. He remembered the way in which he had worked in teams at the ad agency. Why not hire a cowriter to collaborate with him on writing all the books he wanted to write? Once again, his publisher Little, Brown and Company didn't like the idea at first: most writers can churn out one novel a year. Wouldn't readers be suspicious if their favorite author was writing several books in a year? More important, wouldn't they get tired of seeing his name?

Patterson disagreed. He felt that he had a large reader base that would welcome seeing more books with his name on the covers. He was turning himself into a brand, just as he had done for companies in the past. First, he had to find the right people.

One of those people was Michael Ledwidge, who worked as a doorman in a New York City building. Michael Ledwidge really wanted to write novels, and he knew Patterson's books quite well. He also thought he had a lot in common with the best-selling novelist; like Patterson, Ledwidge had majored in English at Manhattan College. He decided to take a chance and ask Patterson for some advice.

Patterson offered more than that: he agreed to read Ledwidge's manuscript, and then he helped him find a good publisher for the book. Ledwidge wrote three novels, but he never made enough money to write full-time. In fact, he left being a bellman to take a better paying job as a telephone maintenance man.

A few years later, Patterson approached Ledwidge. He wanted to know if Ledwidge would like to cowrite a thriller series with him. They would work together closely. Patterson would send Ledwidge an outline of the book, Ledwidge would write a draft, and they would send it back and forth, fine-tuning it until they were both satisfied with it.

Ledwidge's response? He said, in an interview with *USA Today*, that he agreed "at about the speed of light."

The result was the *Michael Bennett* mystery series, featuring a New York City cop who has ten adopted children. Bennett was another compelling character, one whom readers immediately loved.

PATTERSON'S WRITING ROUTINE

Even though he had become a multimillionaire, James Patterson did not give himself a break. His writing routine is one of the most fascinating things about him. It's quite rigorous: he writes every day of the week, 365 days a year. He wakes up at 5:30 A.M., does some small tasks around the house, and

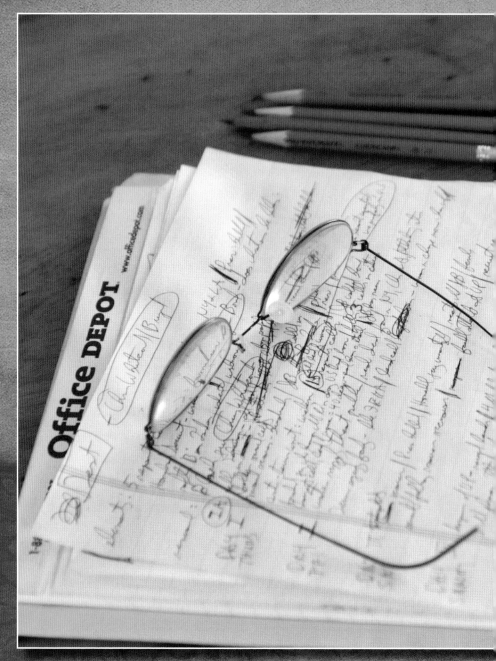

Working with pencil and paper is Patterson's preferred method of writing. He avoids typing or using a computer when he is being creative. Instead, an assistant types up his handwritten pages.

then writes for an hour. Sometimes, he will spend time drafting an outline for a new novel or work on a book revision. Around 7 A.M., he will take a short break and go out for a walk. In Florida, where he lives, he can enjoy consistently good weather year-round. When he returns, he writes until noon.

He avoids modern technology. He could probably write and edit faster were he using a computer, but he doesn't use one. He doesn't even have one in his writing office in his home. Instead, he writes on tablets, with sharpened pencils, and he gives his handwritten pages to an assistant to type up.

Patterson feels he has to "protect" his writing time because he is so busy with other commitments. For example, in any given day, he might have to meet with or take phone calls

COWRITING

One of the most interesting parts of Patterson's writing routine is his process of working with coauthors. Patterson will often draft a detailed outline for a new book; sometimes his outlines are as long as eighty pages. He sends the outline to his coauthor, who will then write it out more fully into a draft of either several chapters or even the whole book. The manuscript is sent back to Patterson, who will read it and revise it carefully, making sure it flows the way he wishes. He wants to ensure, in the end, that when the book is published, he will be proud to see his name on the cover—and that his fans will be satisfied that they have purchased another fast-paced, exciting Patterson novel.

from a coauthor, his publishers, a movie producer, his agent, and others. He has to make sure that the "business" part of being a successful writer does not interfere with his actual ability to write.

Because he writes several novels a year, he always has dozens of projects that are in progress. Around his home office, he has stacks of manuscripts piled on tables. Some are outlines for new books, while others are books in progress, while still others are revisions that his coauthors have sent back to him. No wonder Patterson claims that he never suffers from "writer's block"—he never runs out of ideas because there are always so many manuscripts he needs to write.

In addition to the Alex Cross books, the *Women's Murder Club* mysteries, and the *Michael Bennett* books, his many series include the *Confessions* series, the *Private* series, *NYPD Red*, and many others.

Thanks to his disciplined work ethic, Patterson was writing almost ten books a year by the late 1990s. And then, one day, he realized that while millions of people loved to read his books, there was one reluctant reader living right in his home: his son, Jack.

FIVE

INSPIRING A READER

No doubt, when James Patterson thought about his son, Jack—a good student who didn't enjoy reading—he thought about his own childhood. Hadn't Patterson himself been the same kind of kid: smart, good at school, and curious, but one who avoided books as much as possible?

But maybe he'd been that way, he suspected, because he'd never been given any books that interested him very deeply. After all, once he found books he liked to read, during his night shifts at McLean Hospital, his passion for books had been ignited. In fact, reading had changed the entire course of his life. Patterson had an idea, and he was determined to make it work.

A NEW MARKET

Maybe Jack and other kids his age needed that same inspiration: books they couldn't put down. Not every book is a good book. It was the job of teachers, parents, and even authors themselves to get kids to enjoy reading. "There are millions of kids who have never read a book that they liked, and that is a national disgrace," Patterson said in an interview with the *New York Times*. He decided that he would play his part.

James Patterson is married to Susan (Sue) Solie. They have one child, their son Jack. Here, the Pattersons are photographed at the 2012 premiere of *Alex Cross*, starring Tyler Perry.

After all, he had succeeded in persuading his own son to love to read. The summer plan when Jack was eight – in which Patterson told him he did not have to complete his chores, but he did have to read for a set time period every day – had worked. Though he was unhappy about it at first, Jack Patterson read twelve books by the end of summer vacation. Jack soon became an avid reader, who enjoyed many genres, from classic works of literature to mysteries and adventures.

Patterson was doing what experts suggest: requiring kids to read, but making sure they enjoy the material. Reading on a daily basis helps kids and adults alike to build up the endurance to read. Once they read a lot, they will be able to read better and faster.

Another trick had been to provide Jack with space and support, and then to put the right kind of book into his hands. In an interview with the *Chicago Tribune*, Patterson said, "It's so important to get books to kids that will turn them on to reading. And it's the responsibility of parents—not the schools—to get the light to go off."

Patterson next decided that he would write the kinds of books his son would love to read. From that notion, the ideas for several young adult books were born. This tough mystery writer was about to take on kid's books.

Many writers who have a reputation for one kind of book would have trouble switching to a different, new audience. One might imagine how tough it would be for Patterson, who was known for thrillers and action-adventures, to begin writing for school-aged children.

But it wasn't, thanks to Patterson's avid, vibrant imagination. Patterson's adult books feature characters who are not perfect; they are likeable, but they have problems. He used the same formula to create his young adult characters.

I FUNNY

For example, one of Patterson's most popular series is the *I Funny* books, featuring the character of middle school student Jamie Grimm, who uses a wheelchair. Jamie is a kid who has lived through real tragedy: his mother, father, and little sister were killed in a car crash. Jamie survived the accident, but he was paralyzed from the waist down, and he has now been sent to live with his aunt's family in Long Beach, New York. His relatives, the Kosgrovs, don't treat him very well; his cousin Stevie is the school bully, and his aunt and uncle rarely smile. They also don't seem to be very considerate of the fact that Jamie has to use a wheelchair. In fact, Jamie lives in the family garage, which has been turned into a bedroom for him, although it's a cold and uncomfortable one. However, it's wheelchair accessible: he can exit and enter his room from the driveway, just by opening the garage door.

How does Jamie survive all the terrible things that have happened to him? Through his sense of humor. He is also desperate for people to treat him like they would anyone else, not like a person in a wheelchair. In one scene from *I Funny*, his cousin Stevie threatens to punch him and then actually does it:

> Kosgrov decks me. I mean, he socks me so hard I end up flat on my back like a tipped-over turtle (minus the kicking legs). […] Lying on the ground, staring up at the sky with parking-lot gravel in my hair, I feel that I have finally arrived.
> Stevie Kosgrov punched me just like I was a *regular, normal* kid.
> He didn't call me gimp or crip or Wheelie McFeelie. He just slugged me in the gut and laughed hysterically when I toppled over backward.

Jamie adds later, "This is progress." He wants to be treated like anybody else, so he feels almost grateful when Stevie punches him without feeling sorry for him.

Jamie's sense of humor is the shield he uses to face the world's difficulties. In the novel, he decides to enter a contest for the Planet's Funniest Kid, and the jokes he writes are ones that make fun of how people treat him. "As you know, I'm not handicapped. I'm 'differently abled,'" he says in one of his stand-up routines. Looking at the audience, he delivers the punch line: "That's why I feel so sorry for you guys. You're all so 'ordinarily abled.' Bor-ring."

James Patterson believes passionately in encouraging kids to read. In 2013, he was a guest speaker at the Stuart-Hobson Middle School in Washington, DC. Patterson's books for kids are a departure from his mysteries.

RAFE KATCHADORIAN

Patterson's decision to create a strong, heroic main character who happens to be disabled is refreshing. However, most of the characters in his young adult books have challenges that they need to overcome. For example, another popular character he created is Rafe Katchadorian, the hero of *Middle School: The Worst Years of My Life.* Rafe is a middle schooler who is quite unpopular. He spends his day at middle school avoiding bullies, staying as far away from annoying teachers (such as one English teacher whom he names the Dragon Lady) as possible, and pining after a popular girl named Jeanne Galletta.

One day, Rafe decides that he will never be popular, so he may as well be notorious. His plan, what he calls his "Big Idea," is to break every rule in the *Hills Village Middle School Code of Conduct*. "This was the best idea anyone ever had in the whole history of middle school," he says. "In the whole history of ideas! Not only was it going to help me get through the year, I thought, it might also just save my life here at Hills Village."

The critics loved the complicated character of Rafe Katchadorian, who doesn't want to behave badly; he just simply doesn't know how else to handle such a terrible time in sixth grade. While the

RAFE'S KID SISTER

Rafe is such a popular character, and his family so likeable, that his little sister, Georgia Katchadorian (named after the painter Georgia O'Keefe), now has her own series as well. The first book in that series is titled *My Brother Is a Big, Fat Liar*, in which Georgia is determined to make herself known at Hills Village Middle School to compensate for her brother, who had a disastrous reputation. Georgia wants to be popular, and she has even made a bet with Rafe that she will be.

school's students and teachers think he's wild, Rafe really does care about his little sister, his mother, and his best friend, an artist he names Leonardo the Silent. Later in the first book, the reader learns that Leo the Silent, whom nobody else can see, is really Rafe's imaginary friend. In fact, when he was a baby, Rafe had a twin brother who died. His name was Leonardo, named after Leonardo DaVinci. Rafe himself is named after Raphael Sanzio da Urbino, the great Renaissance painter. The *New York Times* said, "Rafe is the bad boy with a heart of gold," while *Publishers Weekly* said, "Patterson artfully weaves a … thought-provoking tale of childhood coping

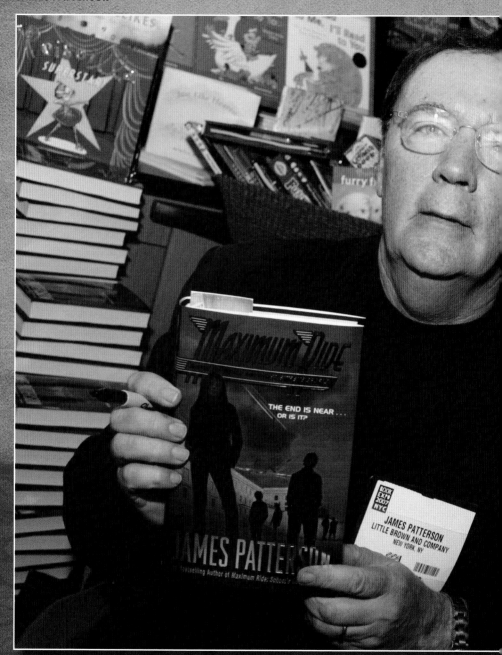

Maximum Ride is yet another successful young adult series created by James Patterson. It features a group of teens who have a unique ability that all kids have dreamed of: they can fly!

mechanisms and everyday school and family realities."

Rafe is a young character who grapples with problems that will be familiar to middle school children. Patterson excels, as the critics note, at understanding and portraying everyday challenges for young people in a realistic way. Every American child has experienced problems at school, including bullies, the urge to be popular, difficult teachers, and the feeling of liking a person who doesn't return the feeling.

MAXIMUM RIDE

Patterson has also created books for young readers that present extraordinary, even fantastical, challenges for this age group. For example, another popular series he created are the *Maximum Ride* novels, which are geared toward older teenaged readers. Maximum Ride, better known as Max, is fourteen years old. She has an unusual name, as well as an unusual skill: because she is part-bird, fly. So can her friends, Fang, Iggy, Nudge, and Angel, who are part of her "flock."

The members of the flock fly around New York City, avoiding people who want to kidnap them. During their adventures, Max realizes that her mission in life is to save the world.

The first book of the series, *Max: The Angel Experiment*, opens the way a typical James Patterson books does: in the middle of the action, or *en medias res.* The opening lines of chapter one are:

> The funny thing about facing imminent death is that it really snaps everything else into perspective. Take right now, for instance.
> *Run! Come on, run! You know you can do it!*
> I gulped deep lungfuls of air. My brain was on hyperdrive; I was racing for my life. My one goal was to escape. Nothing else mattered.

Patterson follows his own advice to get kids to read: give them books that they can't put down, starting right from the first page.

The copyright to the *Maximum Ride* books are not under Patterson's name but under the name "SueJack," which suggests that Patterson found a couple of cowriters right in his household: his wife, Susan Solie, and his son, Jack.

A WRITING WIZARD

Another series of wild, fantastical adventures are told in Patterson's *Treasure Hunters* series. The books follow the adventures of the Kidd family, who grow up helping their parents excavate lost treasures. There are four siblings: Tommy, Storm, and twins Bick and Beck. One day, their mom disappears in Cyprus, and then their dad vanishes while they are in the Caribbean. Now, the Kidd siblings are on their own, but readers will be startled by how capable these young people are at surviving: after all, they've grown up with adventurous parents, and they know how to handle themselves. Determined to find and recover their parents, the Kidds experience many wild adventures, such as battling pirates and avoiding a rival treasure hunter.

Patterson donated hundreds of thousands of copies of his books to schools across the United States. It is one of his missions to get good books into the hands of children, to encourage them to read for pleasure.

In the *Treasure Hunters* series, Patterson also included many illustrations. The *Middle School* and *I Funny* books are also illustrated, but not as much as *Treasure Hunters*. Juliana Neufeld, an illustrator and artist who lives in Canada, is one of the people with whom Patterson worked to give visual life to the *Treasure Hunters* books. The *Treasure Hunters* books make it easy for young children to transition to longer chapter books because of the illustrations.

WITCH AND WIZARD

James Patterson has also written books for older kids, including for teenagers. One of his most popular series for this group is the *Witch and Wizard* books. His co-author in this series is Gabrielle Charbonnet, a

Louisiana-based writer who has several young adult books of her own.

The *Witch and Wizard* books are fantastical adventures set in the future. Whitford Allgood and his sister Wisteria (known as Whit and Wisty) are in trouble—they are being accused of possessing powers of evil. They are arrested by a vain fellow student named Byron Swain, who claims that they are a witch and a wizard. Before they are taken away to prison by the authorities, Whit and Wisty are given a drumstick and a book by their parents. In prison, the siblings are clued in about who they really are: they are the Liberators, who must save the world. They are introduced to several characters who help them in their journey, including a mysterious figure named the One Who Is the One. While in prison, they are introduced to new worlds—the Shadowland and the Freeland, in which they begin to understand their special powers. Wisty can create fire, while Whit has healing powers and can mentally manipulate objects. Using their newfound magic, they strive to reconnect with their parents as well as help fulfill their destinies as the Liberators.

Even though they are written for older children, like most of Patterson's books, the *Witch and Wizard* books nevertheless have very short chapters. They are narrated by the two siblings, in the first person, and they end in a Patterson-style cliffhanger. For

Many of James Patterson's books are written in conjunction with coauthors. Patterson has enjoyed teamwork since his days at the J. Walter Thompson ad agency in New York City.

example, consider the end of chapter one, narrated by Whit:

> Almost faster than I could comprehend, two armed squads detached them-selves from the phalanx and sprinted across the lawn like commandos, one run-ning around the back of the house, the other taking posi-tion in the front.
>
> I jumped away from the window. I could tell they weren't here to protect me and my family. I had to warn Mom, Dad, Wisty –
>
> But just as I started to yell, the front door was knocked off its hinges.

Despite some reviews claiming that the first book contained a lot of backstory and explanation, the series has been popular, as have all of Patterson's books. The series has grown to include the sequels *Witch and Wizard: The Gift*, *Witch and Wizard: The Fire*, *Witch and Wizard: The Kiss*, and *Witch and Wizard: The Lost*.

As part of his speech at the Stuart-Hobson Middle School in Washington, DC, Patterson holds a book signing for students. He enjoys meeting children and learning their interests, all of which help him write books that they will enjoy.

DANIEL X

Patterson's *Daniel X* series also features a teenaged character who has a mission: to save the world as he knows it. Daniel is a teenage boy with a major secret: he's an extraterrestrial. In other words, he's an alien. He's also an orphan, whose parents have been killed by another alien. Daniel has landed on Earth, and as a nonhuman, he has superpower abilities, which put him in the position to be able to save Earth from other, evil aliens. The books have short chapters and cliffhanger endings, such as this one from *The Dangerous Days of Daniel X:* "'The aliens are here,' I whispered, and reached up and clicked off the basement light. I prepared to be eaten, or maybe worse."

Steve Johnson, writing about James Patterson in the *Chicago Tribune*, said that Patterson's young adult novels are "humor-laden books about

PICTURES ARE JUST FINE

Interestingly, Patterson has received some criticism for the heavy use of illustrations in his books. The books, his critics say, are "easy reading" because of all the pictures, but Patterson scoffs at the implication that the books are too simple. "They're not dumb books," he told reporter Steve Johnson in 2014. "There's nothing wrong with pictures. Movies are all pictures. I don't know if you've noticed, but museums have a lot of pictures in them. Pictures are just fine."

alienated or misfit teens." That may be part of the appeal of these books for young readers: everyone, in his or her childhood, has had moments of loneliness, of feeling misunderstood. All of Patterson's main characters—Jamie Grimm, Daniel X, Whit and Wisty, Rafe and Georgia—are struggling to be understood and accepted, despite their differences. They must learn to cope with the special talent or uniqueness that makes them unlike the other kids in their societies.

And he seems to understand kids very well. In fact, in 2014, Johnson's newspaper, the *Chicago Tribune,* awarded Patterson its annual Young Adult Literary Award. Patterson was recognized for this award in part because of the fact that he donated twenty-eight thousand copies of his books to Chicago's public schoolchildren, recognizing that many children do not read because they cannot afford to purchase books of their own.

SEVEN

READ, KIDDO, READ!

In 2015, James Patterson teamed up with Scholastic, the widely known children's book publisher and bookseller, to announce a new campaign: he would donate $1.5 million to American school libraries. Libraries could apply for grants of up to $10,000 to improve or expand their spaces and make reading more enjoyable for children. Scholastic has made the deal even better by pledging additional book club points for winning libraries to use for the purchase of books and classroom reading supplies.

THE IMPORTANCE OF LIBARIES

Why is Patterson doing this? It's not just because he's a nice person with a fondness for libraries (he has cherished memories of his mother taking him to the Newburgh public library on a regular basis). It's because libraries have been underfunded for years due to tight school budgets.

Patterson told the *Washington Post* that he hopes that when school libraries receive the money, it will "lift morale." He added: "It allows the local school library to get publicity in the community, if it hopes to do so. And, most important of all, what I'm trying to do is shine a light on a much larger problem."

That "much larger" problem is the fact that young children do not read for enjoyment as much as they used to. Patterson worries about something that has been well documented: many kids, for the last decade, spend more time on electronic screen devices and not in the pages of a book. In fact, it has been documented by organizations like the National Endowment for the Arts that most Americans in general do not read regularly. They are too distracted by other forms of entertainment, says the NEA report *Reading At Risk: A Survey of Literary Reading in America*. The report explains why: "Reading a book requires a degree of active attention and engagement. Indeed, reading itself is a progressive skill that depends on years of education and practice. By contrast, most electronic media … require no more than passive participation." In other words, reading

In 2014, Patterson participated in the LEARN project, sponsored by the NBA. He attended the event, which celebrated the importance of reading, at the Joseph S. Clark High School in New Orleans, Louisiana.

demands more of our time and attention, which is why people avoid it.

Many proponents of technology argue that thousands, even millions, of books are available as e-books, on devices like Kindles, Nooks, and other tablets. Patterson, who famously avoids technology, believes that kids need to read "bound books."

"Kids have not made the switch to reading books on phones, tablets or even e-readers," he said in an interview with the *Washington Post*. "It isn't useful for anyone to go on the Internet and see 2 to 4 million titles. It is useful to have human beings to talk to and help guide you to exactly the kind of book you're looking for or hope to find." This is why supporting local school libraries has become a priority for the best-selling author.

A DISAPPOINTING OUTREACH ENDEAVOR

The truth is, however, that Patterson has long been dedicated to the cause of getting children to read. Perhaps this enthusiasm was inspired by his own success with getting his son, Jack, to become an avid reader, but there is no doubt that more kids are reading today because of efforts that Patterson has made.

Patterson believes that it is the responsibility of the parents to encourage children to read. Teachers and others can help, too, but Patterson learned firsthand, with his son, Jack, that parents can find books their kids will want to read.

At one point, the best-selling author established a foundation called the James Patterson PageTurner Awards, which was designed to donate money to schools, teachers, and library systems. However, Patterson canceled the effort and shut down the organization in 2008 when he realized not enough people were applying for the grants he was offering. The fact that not enough people applied for the money shocked him. In an interview with *Publishers Weekly*, he said, jokingly, "It was

BOOK DONATIONS

Patterson also knows that many children and parents cannot afford good books. He has offered a solution for this problem as well: he regularly donates books to schools in New York, Chicago, and his home state of Florida.

For example, in New York, every sixth grade student started the summer of 2014 with a new book to read. Patterson donated forty-five thousand copies of his newest book, *Middle School: The Worst Years of My Life*, starring his loveable but trouble-seeking character Rafe Katchadorian. Patterson's generous act was highly praised, and he said, as reported in *USA Today*, "These students have the potential to do great things, and supporting and nurturing that potential is our most important job as parents, and as citizens."

like, 'hay-aaaay! We're trying to give money away here!' It was kind of funny. All these organizations are dying for money, and we couldn't get enough people to apply."

James Patterson gives a talk at the BookExpo publishing convention in 2015 to promote his latest book. His books are heavily promoted at this annual event of booksellers, and he is one of its stars.

But it did not take James Patterson long to think up another approach to getting kids to read. In 2011, Patterson established a website, ReadKiddoRead (www.ReadKiddoRead.com), which helps parents find books that their kids will enjoy. The site is organized into age groups: illustrated books for ages 0 to 8 (yes, even infants can be read to!), then books for 6 and up, 8 and up, and 10 and up. ReadKiddoRead offers reviews of most books to help parents make good choices as well. The site also features an article for parents titled "10 Tips to Get Your Kids Reading," in which Patterson emphasizes that inspiring a love of books is a job for parents, not teachers. One of the tips Patterson offers parents is, "Model reading with your child. Read the same books together, and talk about them."

BOOK BUCKS

Patterson is also concerned about the fact that many college students cannot afford to pay for their college textbooks, some of which can cost hundreds of dollars. According to a 2014 study by the U.S. Public Interest Research Group, the price of college textbooks has increased almost 82 percent in the last ten years, costing students approximately $1,200 a year. To help alleviate some of the burden on college students, Patterson established the James Patterson College Book Bucks (originally called Dollars for Scholars), an award program that gives away certificates worth between $250 and $1,000. In order to win, students have to write a short essay that answers the question: "How has your favorite book inspired you toward what you'd like to do in life?"

The 2014 first-place winner wrote about Orson Scott Card's novel *Finder's Game* and how it inspired him to want to teach. The entry was published on James Patterson's website: "This book taught me the power of teachers, and the lesson was instantly reinforced by my life. My teachers have had an extraordinary impact on me. … A teacher's power may not be obvious, but it is great." (Patterson has established similar programs for schoolchildren, called Summer Book Bucks, in which kids who pledge to read four books over the summer can enter a sweepstakes to win $50 certificates to be used to buy more books.

DEFENDER OF THE BOOK

O ther groups have benefited from Patterson's generosity and devotion to the idea of inspiring people to read. For example, Patterson regularly donates copies of his books to U.S. military personnel. In 2014, Patterson and his publisher, Little, Brown and Company, donated 180,000 hardcover versions of Patterson's adult novels to U.S. troops. The books were distributed by Patterson's partner organizations in the program, Coalition to Salute America's Heroes and Feed the Children. According to an article in *USA Today*, with the latest donation, Patterson has given away almost 680,000 copies of his books over the years to American armed forces.

Independent bookstores have received grants from James Patterson to improve

their places of business. The only criteria Patterson had for stores to apply for his grants was that the stores had to have a children's book section. He donated more than $1 million to approximately 178 stores, which are suffering because of the dominance of major bookstore chains like Barnes & Noble as well as Amazon.com, the online retailer, which is responsible for 40 percent of all book sales. Patterson wants to revive the idea of parents taking their children into a local bookshop to purchase

Candice Cohen owns the Palm Beach Book Store, in James Patterson's hometown. She recently received a grant from his foundation to fund projects that will promote the bookshop.

books for their children to read. In an interview about his initiative with the Associated Press, he said, "It's crazy that so few people are buying books for their kids."

He has also extended his generosity beyond the American borders. He contributed 50,000 pounds (or $75,000) to British and Irish schools to help launch the World Book Day Awards. These awards will fund five schools and help them buy books for their libraries. The schools apply for the awards by answering the question "Why can't we live without books?" in any media form they wish (video, text, song, or other form). Over 800 schools all over Great Britain and Ireland applied, and many bookstores also participated.

NOT WITHOUT HIS CRITICS

For every good thing James Patterson has done to promote reading, there are still critics who call him, as the *Boston Globe* reported that Stephen King did, "a terrible writer." Other critics have charged that Patterson writes easy and unchallenging books, and that his writing style—with its sparse description and very short chapters—is too simplistic.

However, Patterson does not seem to care what critics have to say. He cares more about his readers, who are buying his books by the millions. As *Boston*

Globe reporter James Sullivan said, "You don't sell nearly 300 million books—heck, you don't sell 10,000—without doing something right by your readers."

PATTERSON NOVELS ON THE BIG AND SMALL SCREENS

Patterson has also made the leap from the page to the screen. In 2012, a new Alex Cross movie was released, starring Tyler Perry as the psychologist and police detective. It didn't do very well, in terms of the critical response. Some viewers felt that Perry was the problem, while others felt that the film script was weak.

However, 2012 was not the first time a movie was made based on a Patterson novel. In fact, Alex Cross was portrayed in two movies in the late 1990s and early 2000s by renowned actor Morgan Freeman. In 2010, Patterson's novel *Sundays at Tiffany's* was turned

The author who once took inspiration from *The Exorcist* is now no stranger to having movies made from his novels. A new Alex Cross movie was released in 2012, and many others are in the works for both the big and small screens.

into a TV movie starring Alyssa Milano. Furthermore, the *Women's Murder Club* books were turned into a TV miniseries, starring Angie Harmon. The book series was also turned into a video game by the Flood Light Games company. Patterson's *Private* books also inspired a TV series. His young adult books seem to be heading for screen adaptations as well. In 2015, it was announced that *Maximum Ride* would be produced as a film. He also recently signed a deal with CBS TV to turn some of his books into TV shows and movies.

Maybe the transition to the screen is not as difficult as it is with other books because Patterson's novels are so plot-driven. The story matters more than anything, according to Patterson. He is not trying to write books that will change the world; he just wants to entertain people.

In an interview with *Time* magazine, he said, "I'm a storyteller. There are thousands of people who don't like what I do. Fortunately, there are millions who do."

A NEW VENTURE

In 2015, Patterson made an important announcement at BookExpo America, the country's largest trade book fair. He was launching Jimmy Patterson, a new imprint for his publisher, Little, Brown and

JAMES PATTERSON AND HOLLYWOOD

Patterson strives to be involved with the production process of the movie and TV show adaptations of his books, especially because he has so many years of experience in producing TV commercials and other forms of media. He will often participate in writing the screenplay or script for a movie based on one of his books.

He has been eager to see his books turned into films. Unfortunately, very few of Patterson-inspired movies have been regarded very highly by movie critics. However, Patterson wants to change this; he hopes that some of his books will be scripted into excellent movies that receive critical acclaim, especially because he is such an avid moviegoer himself. He enjoys spending his evenings having dinner and watching a film, and he goes to the theater regularly to see all the major films released every year. He told a *Hollywood Reporter* interviewer, "I'm a movie theater freak. Love 'em." In recent years, he has been writing short reviews of other films on his website, www.JamesPatterson.com.

He has also established his own marketing company, James Patterson Entertainment (JPE) to help market the James Patterson brand, including how to help make the transition between Patterson's novels to the small screen (television) or the big screen (movies). Patterson also needs the help because he has offers and deals from other media companies, like Netflix, which paid to run other Patterson-inspired movies and shows for its customers.

Company. Jimmy Patterson would be a children's imprint, releasing eight to twelve young adult books per year. The books are written by Patterson and other authors, with Patterson overseeing all acquisitions.

Perhaps most important, all proceeds from the sales of Jimmy titles go to Patterson's literacy efforts. Money will be directed to scholarships for teachers, helping independent bookstores, the distribution of books to underprivileged communities,

Best-selling author James Patterson's books are enjoyed by people from all backgrounds and all stations in life. Every year, he continues to deliver novels that his fans enjoy, cover to cover.

and funding school libraries. The imprint is a way to not only produce great books for kids and young adults—it's also another way for Patterson to meet his goal of getting kids to read.

Just as he once applied his expertise to selling toys and cars while working as an ad executive, James Patterson has, in the last two decades, developed a brand for his books. A James Patterson book is recognizable to a customer shopping at either a bookstore or a supermarket (Patterson's books are among the few best-selling titles that make it into WalMart or grocery store aisles)—it has a distinctive cover, it has short chapters, the action begins right away, and the story is riveting.

Most of all, as millions of readers around the world will attest, one just cannot put down a James Patterson book.

ON JAMES PATTERSON

Birth date: March 22, 1947
Birthplace: Newburgh, New York
Current residence: Palm Beach, Florida
Parents: Charles and Isabelle Patterson
First book: *The Thomas Berryman Number* (published in 1976)
Marital status: Married to Susan Solie Patterson
Children: Jack Patterson
Education: Manhattan College (BA, English), Vanderbilt University (MA, English)
Employer: J. Walter Thompson
World record: Most hardcover fiction best-selling titles by a single author: 63 (*Guinness Book of World Records*)

ON JAMES PATTERSON'S WORK

James Patterson's Books for Young Readers

Middle School Series
#1 *New York Times* Best Seller

Hills Village *Middle School* is supposed to be a great
place, but Rafe Katchadorian is having a rough
start. For starters, there's a code of conduct
filled with rules that beg to be broken, and his
friend Leo pushes him to make trouble. Rafe's
home life isn't much better: his mother's boy-
friend has moved into Rafe's house and is
making family life difficult. The series follows
Rafe through various adventures, where he
experiences zany summer camps, art school,
outdoor survival excursions, and managing both
bullies and friends.

**Winner of the 2012 Children's Choice
Book Awards:**
**Author of the Year for *Middle School: The Worst
Years of My Life***

Books in this series include:

Middle School: The Worst Years of My Life (2011,
  coauthor: Chris Tebbetts)
Middle School: Get Me Out of Here (2012, coauthor:
  Chris Tebbetts)
Middle School: My Brother Is a Big Fat Liar (2013,
  coauthor: Lisa Papademetriou)
*Middle School: How I Survived Bullies, Broccoli, and
  Snake Hill* (2013, coauthor: Chris Tebbetts)
Middle School: Save Rafe! (2014, coauthor: Chris
  Tebbetts)

Maximum Ride Series
#1 *New York Times* Best Seller

Max seems like an average teenaged girl, with average friends, except that they're part-birds. Max
  and her buddies, Fang, Iggy, Nudge, the
  Gasman, and Angel (known as the Flock), were
  actually created in a science lab. Now they've
  managed to escape, except that it feels like
  everyone is out to get them. Max is trying to
  both stay out of the clutches of the Erasers, who
  hunt for human-bird hybrids, as well as help her
  family. On top of all that, she searches for the
  meaning in her life. What is her destiny? Why
  was she created in the first place? She and the
  Flock realize that their fate is linked to the fate of
  the world.

It was announced in 2015 that Maximum Ride *will be released as a motion picture, produced by Ari Arad and James Patterson.*

Books in this series include:

Maximum Ride: The Angel Experiment (2007)

Maximum Ride: School's Out Forever (2007)

Maximum Ride: Saving the World and Other Extreme Sports (2007)

Maximum Ride: The Final Warning (2009)

Max: A Maximum Ride Novel (2010)

Fang: A Maximum Ride Novel (2011)

Angel: A Maximum Ride Novel (2012)

Nevermore: The Final Maximum Ride Adventure (2014)

Maximum Ride Forever (2015)

Witch and Wizard Series

#1 *New York Times* Best Seller

Whit and Wisty Allgood, brother and sister, are arrested one day for something that is considered a crime by the new government: they possess magical abilities. Nobody is more surprised than they are to know they're being tried as a witch and a wizard. Before they are hauled off to jail, having been condemned by one of their schoolmates, Whit and Wisty are given a book and a drumstick by their parents. Later they learn the true powers they possess. They also discover their mission:

they must help stop the new government, led by a mysterious figure known as the One Who Is the One.

Books in this series include:
Witch and Wizard (2009, with Gabrielle Charbonnet)
Witch and Wizard: The Gift (2010, coauthor: Ned Rust)
Witch and Wizard: The Fire (2011, coauthor: Jill Dembowski)
Witch and Wizard: The Kiss (2013 , coauthor: Jill Dembowski)
Witch and Wizard: The Lost (2014, coauthor: Emily Raymond)

I Funny Series
#1 *New York Times* Best Seller

Jamie Grimm is on a mission to become the funniest stand-up comic in America. There's only one problem: he's confined to a wheelchair after a terrible accident. But even though his disability bothers everyone else, Jamie doesn't want it to stop him from achieving his goal. He lives with his aunt and uncle and his cousin—who happens to be the school's biggest bully—but Jamie won't give up his dream to win the Planet's Funniest Kid Comic Contest. The books feature wonderful illustrations as well as text.

Books in this series include:
I Funny (2013, coauthor: Chris Grabenstein)
I Even Funnier (2013, coauthor: Chris Grabenstein)
I Totally Funniest (2015, coauthor: Chris Grabenstein)

Awards
Library of Congress Literacy Awards: 2013 Champion
    of Young Readers
Children's Choice Book Awards: Author of the Year
    2010 and 2012
National Parenting Publications Honors Awards
Guinness Book of World Records: Most Number of #1
    New York Times Best Sellers
International Reading Association's Young Adults'
    Choices Booklist
American Library Association "Teens Top Ten" Pick
London Times Book Sense Children's Pick
Edgar Award from the Mystery Writers of America,
    1977

Review of *I Funny*: "The broad humor that runs throughout this heavily illustrated story from Patterson and Grabenstein masks personal pain, demonstrating resiliency in the face of tragedy."—*Publisher's Weekly*

Review of *Middle School*: *The Worst Years of My Life*: "Rafe lashes out against an establishment that is designed against him and a shattered family unit, and it's hard to push past his defense systems. But once through, readers will discover the best kind of child: one that is intelligent, artistic and brave."—*Kirkus Reviews*

Review of *Maximum Ride*: "A group of genetically enhanced kids who can fly and have other unique talents are on the run from part-human, part-wolf predators called Erasers in this exciting SF thriller that's not wholly original but is still a compelling read."—*School Library Journal*

Review of *Treasure Hunters*: "From kidnapping to underwater speargun fights, action is the name of the game here, bolstered by bits of comedy. Although the premise and plot are wholly unconvincing, the fast-paced, first-person narrative is entertaining. With 10 treasures (not to mention two parents) waiting to be discovered, it looks like a new series is on the horizon."—*BookList*

1947 James Patterson is born in Newburgh, New York.

1971 He begins working at J. Walter Thompson as a copywriter.

1976 He publishes *The Thomas Berryman Number*, his first novel.

1977 His is awarded the Edgar Award for his first novel.

1993 He publishes his first blockbuster, *Along Came a Spider*.

1996 He retires from J. Walter Thompson to write full-time.

1997 He marries Susan Solie.

1998 His son, Jack, is born.

2005 He establishes the James Patterson PageTurner Awards to promote reading.

2008 He establishes a website, www.ReadKiddoRead.com, to help parents and young people find appropriate books.

2010 He becomes the first author to sell over 1 million e-books.

2014 It is estimated that Patterson's books have sold 300 million copies.

AD An abbreviation for "advertisement," which can take many forms: billboard, TV commercial, short film, newspaper and magazine, and others.

AD AGENCY A company that is hired to produce commercials, print ads, or signs that promote its clients' products or services.

AGENT A person who works for the writer to help him or her sell book manuscripts to publishers. An agent can also help negotiate contracts for a book to be turned into an audiobook, a movie, an e-book, and other forms of media.

BEST SELLER A book that sells a large number of copies.

BLOCKBUSTER A book that has sold one million copies.

CHARACTER The fictional person in a novel or story.

COMMERCIAL A short film, about thirty to sixty seconds long, that is shown on television to promote a product or service.

COMMERCIAL FICTION A work of fiction that is entertaining but easily put into a category, such as "mystery," "thriller," "romance," "science fiction," and so on.

COPYWRITER A writer who writes words for a specific purpose or to fill a certain need, such as words needed on a product package, on a website, or for a magazine advertisement.

FANTASY A subgenre of fiction in which the imaginary people and/or places being described could not exist in real life.

FICTION A genre of literature that is told in prose, usually short stories, novels, or novellas, that describes the actions and problems of imaginary people.

GENRE A category of writing, such as fiction, drama, poetry, or nonfiction. Within each genre, there are subgenres: fiction can be further categorized into mystery, romance, thriller, science fiction, fantasy, and more.

NOVEL A work of fiction that is usually between 50,000 and 100,000 words in length.

PLOT The events that take place in a work of fiction.

SCREEN ADAPTATION The process of rewriting a work of literature into a script for a film or TV show.

SERIES A number of novels that describe the experiences of the same set of characters.

THRILLER A subgenre of fiction that is action-packed and marked by suspense.

VALEDICTORIAN The highest-ranking student, academically, in a graduating high school or college class.

YOUNG ADULT (YA) A publishing term that describes novels or books for whom the target audience is children ages 12 to18. A young adult novel may be shorter in length than a typical novel (20,000 to 60,000 words).

Association of Canadian Publishers (ACP)
174 Spadina Avenue, Suite 306 Toronto, ON M5T
        2C2
Canada
(416) 487-6116
Website: http://publishers.ca/
The ACP tries to emphasize the importance of read-
        ing and books, especially for Canadian
        English-language books.

Canadian Authors Association (CAA)
6 West Street N, Suite 203
Orillia, ON L3V 5B8
Canada
(705) 325-3926
Website: http://canadianauthors.org/national/
The CAA helps emerging writers develop their skills
        and find ways to become published.

Children's Book Council (CBC)
54 West 39th Street, 14th Floor
New York, NY 10018
(212) 966-1990
Website: http://www.cbcbooks.org/
The CBC is a nonprofit organization that works to
        help book publishers in North America.

The Children's Book Review (CBR)
830 W Route 22, #127

Lake Zurich, IL 60047
Website: http://www.thechildrensbookreview.com/
The CBR is a site that offers a review of all major
    books published for children, as well as inter-
    views with children's book authors and
    illustrators.

Children's Literature Association (ChLA)
1301 W 22nd Street, Suite 202
Oak Brook, IL 60523
(630) 571-4520
Website: http://www.childlitassn.org/
The ChLA promotes the study of children's literature;
    its members are scholars, teachers, librarians,
    and writers.

Mystery Writers of America
1140 Broadway, Suite 1507
New York, NY 10001
(212) 888-8171
Website: https://mysterywriters.org/
    contact-mwa-national-office/
MWA is the premier organization for mystery and
    crime writers, professionals allied to the crime
    writing field, aspiring crime writers, and folks
    who just love to read crime fiction.

Scholastic Reading Club
Scholastic, Inc.

2931 E. McCarty Street
Jefferson City, MO 65101
(800) SCHOLASTIC
Website: https://clubs2.scholastic.com
Scholastic is a major publisher of children's books
and school curricula.

Society of Children's Book Writers and Illustrators
4727 Wilshire Boulevard, Suite 301
Los Angeles, CA 90010
(323) 782-1010
Website: http://www.scbwi.org/
This is a professional organization for authors and
illustrators of children's books. It provides them
with opportunities to learn about the industry
and to network.

Stone Soup, Inc.
Stone Soup Submissions Dept.
P.O. Box 83
Santa Cruz, CA 95063
(800) 447-4569
Website: http://www.stonesoup.com/
Stone Soup is a magazine that is written and illus-
trated by children, ages 8 to 13.

The Writer
25 Braintree Hill Office Park, Suite 404
Braintree, MA 02184
(877) 252-8139

Website: http://www.writermag.com
A magazine for people at all stages of their writing
careers, *The Writer* offers valuable advice,
articles, and contest information.

WEBSITES

Because of the changing nature of Internet links,
Rosen Publishing has developed an online list of
websites related to the subject of this book. This site
is updated regularly. Please use this link to access
this list:

http://www.rosenlinks.com/AAA/Patt

Bell, Cece. *El Deafo.* New York, NY: Harry N. Abrams, 2014.

Benke, Karen. *Lean Write In! Adventures in Creative Writing to Stretch and Surprise Your One-of-a-Kind Mind.* Boston, MA: Roost Books, 2013.

Benke, Karen. *Rip the Page! Adventures in Creative Writing.* Boston, MA: Roost Books, 2010.

Capacchione, Lucia. *The Creative Journal for Teens: Making Friends with Yourself.* Pompton Plains, NJ: Career Press, 2008.

Going, K. L. *Writing and Selling the Young Adult Novel.* Cincinnati, OH: Writer's Digest Books, 2008.

Holm, Jennifer. *The Fourteenth Goldfish.* New York, NY: Random House Books for Young Readers, 2014.

Joyce, James. *A Portrait of the Artist as a Young Man.* New York, NY: Penguin, 2003.

Joyce, James. *Ulysses.* New York, NY: Vintage, 1986.

Kinney, Jeff. *Diary of a Wimpy Kid.* New York, NY: Amulet, 2007.

Kole, Mary. *Writing Irresistable Kidlit: The Ultimate Guide to Crafting Fiction for Young Adult and Middle Grade Readers.* Cincinnati, OH: Writer's Digest Books, 2012.

Krull, Kathleen, and David Leonard. *Women Who Broke the Rules: Judy Blume.* New York, NY: Bloomsbury, 2015.

Levine, Gail Carson. *Writer to Writer: From Think to Ink.* New York, NY: HarperCollins, 2014.

Levine, Gail Carson. *Writing Magic: Creating Stories that Fly.* New York, NY: HarperCollins, 2006.

Marquez, Gabriel Garcia. *Love in the Time of Cholera.* New York, NY: Vintage, 2007.

Marquez, Gabriel Garcia. *One Hundred Years of Solitude.* New York, NY: Harper, 2006.

Peirce, Lincoln. *Big Nate: In a Class By Himself.* New York, NY: HarperCollins, 2010.

Potter, Ellen, et al. *Spilling Ink: A Young Writer's Handbook.* New York, NY: Square Fish Books, 2010.

Russell, Rachel Renée. *Dork Diaries.* New York, NY: Aladdin, 2009.

Selznick, Brian. *The Invention of Hugo Cabret.* New York, NY: Scholastic, 2007.

Semple, Maria. *Where'd You Go, Bernadette?* New York, NY: Back Bay Books, 2013.

Snicket, Lemony. *The Bad Beginning: Or, Orphans! A Series of Unfortunate Events, Book 1.* New York, NY: HarperCollins, 2007.

Telgemeier, Rana. *Drama.* New York, NY: Graphix, 2012.

Telgemeier, Rana. *Sisters.* New York, NY: Graphix, 2014.

Telgemeier, Rana. *Smile.* New York, NY: Graphix, 2010.

Zusak, Markus. *The Book Thief.* New York, NY: Knopf, 2007.

Associated Press. "James Patterson Donating to
    Independent Bookstores." *USA Today*,
    December 15, 2014. Retrieved April 12, 2015
    (http://www.usatoday.com/story/life/
    books/2014/12/15/
    james-patterson-donating-to-independent-book-
    stores/20427143/).

Bidwell, Allie. "Report: High Textbook Prices Have
    College Students Struggling." January 28, 2014.
    U.S. News and World Report. Retrieved April 10,
    2015 (http://www.usnews.com/news/arti-
    cles/2014/01/28/
    report-high-textbook-prices-have-college-stu-
    dents-struggling).

Charles, Ron. "James Patterson Pledges $1.25 Million
    to School Libraries." *Washington Post*, March 9,
    2015. Retrieved April 5, 2015 (http://www.wash-
    ingtonpost.com/blogs/style-blog/wp/2015/03/09/
    james-patterson-wants-to-give-1-25-million-to-
    school-libraries).

Charney, Noah. "How I Write: James Patterson."
    TheDailyBeast.com, January 29, 2014. Retrieved
    April 5, 2015 (http://www.thedailybeast.com/
    articles/2014/01/29/how-i-write-james-patterson.
    html).

City of Newburgh Official Website. Retrieved April
    2015 (http://www.cityofnewburgh-ny.gov/city-
    history/pages/the-post-war-years).

Harvkey, Mike. "Read, Kiddo, Read: James Patterson."

Publishers Weekly, May 23, 2011. Retrieved April 13, 2015 (http://www.publishersweekly.com/pw/by-topic/authors/profiles/article/47370-read-kiddo-read-james-patterson.html).

Higginbotham, Adam. "James Patterson Interview." *Telegraph*, January 27, 2010.

The Hollywood Reporter. "Hollywood's 25 Most Powerful Authors." November 28, 2012. Retrieved April 5, 2015 (http://www.hollywoodre-porter.com/lists/8-james-patterson-394091).

Johnson, Steve. "Patterson's Passion: Getting Kids to Read." *Chicago Tribune*, June 4, 2014. Retrieved April 13, 2015 (http://articles.chicagotribune.com/2014-06-04/entertainment/chi-james-patterson-wants-kids-to-read-20140604_1_james-patterson-independent-bookstores-alex-cross).

Keefe, Patrick Radden. "Welcome to Newburgh, Murder Capital of New York." Retrieved April 1, 2015 (http://nymag.com/news/crimelaw/newburgh-2011-10/).

Lawler, Kelly. "Book Buzz: James Patterson Donates Books to the Troops." *USA Today,* September 15, 2014. Retrieved April 11, 2015 (http://www.usatoday.com/story/life/books/2014/09/15/book-buzz-james-patterson-gives-books-to-the-troops/15659595/).

Lexington Minuteman. Obituary: Isabelle Patterson. January 22, 2010. Retrieved April 13, 2015

(http://www.legacy.com/obituaries/wickedlocal-lexington/obituary.
aspx?n=isabelle-patterson-morris&pid=138772919).

Mahler, Jonathan. "James Patterson, Inc." *New York Times.* January 24, 2010. Retrieved April 2015 (http://www.nytimes.com/2010/01/24/magazine/24patterson-t.html?_r=0).

McClurg, Jocelyn. "Patterson Donates Books to New York City Schools." *USA Today,* June 23, 2014. Retrieved April 13, 2015 (http://www.usatoday.com/story/life/books/2014/06/23/james-patterson-new-york-city-schools-books-giveaway/11266131).

Minzesheimer, Bob. "Publishing juggernaut Patterson keeps rolling along." February 4, 2007. Retrieved April 1, 2015 (http://usatoday30.usatoday.com/life/books/news/2007-02-04-james-patterson_x.htm).

National Endowment for the Arts. "Reading at Risk: A Survey of Literary Reading in America." June 2004. Retrieved April 2015 (http://arts.gov/sites/default/files/ReadingAtRisk.pdf).

NBCNews.com. "James Patterson, Inc: Alex Cross Author on Churning Out Bestsellers." December 18, 2012. Retrieved April 12, 2015 (http://rock-center.nbcnews.com/_news/2012/12/18/15975443-james-patterson-inc-alex-cross-author-on-churning-out-bestsellers?lite).

Patterson, James. "10 Tips to Get Your Kids Reading."
    Retrieved April 2015 (http://readkiddoread.com/
    blogjames-pattersons-10-tips-to-get-your-kids-
    reading).

Patterson, James. *Max: The Angel Experiment.* New
    York, NY: Little, Brown and Company, 2005.

Patterson, James, and Chris Grabenstein. *I Funny: A
    Middle School Story.* New York, NY: Little, Brown
    and Company, 2013.

Patterson, James, and Chris Tebbetts. *Middle School:
    The Worst Year of My Life.* New York, NY: Little,
    Brown and Company, 2011.

Patterson, James, and Gabrielle Charbonnet. *Witch
    and Wizard.* New York, NY: Little, Brown and
    Company, 2011.

Patterson, James, and Michael Ledwidge. *The
    Dangerous Days of Daniel X.* New York, NY: Little,
    Brown and Company, 2010.

Purdum, Todd. "The Henry Ford of Books." *Vanity Fair,*
    January 2015. Retrieved April 2015 (http://www.
    vanityfair.com/culture/2015/01/
    james-patterson-best-selling-author).

St. Patrick's and Our Lady of the Lake. "History of
    Parish." Retrieved April 2015 (http://www.stpat-
    ricksnewburgh.org/index.php?option=com_cont
    ent&view=article&id=74&Itemid=85).

Sullivan, James. "Patterson Keeps Cranking Out
    Novels, Ignoring His Critics." *Boston Globe,*
    January 25, 2014. Retrieved April 1, 2015 (http://
    www.bostonglobe.com/arts/books/2014/01/25/

james-patterson-keeps-cranking-out-his-novels-
and-ignoring-his-critics/bE3dvgtizkvo8viXdUls5N/
story.html).

Time. "10 Questions for James Patterson." July 5,
2010. Retrieved April 1, 2015 (http://content.time.
com/time/magazine/article/0,9171,1999411,00.
html).

Trice, Dawn Turner. "A Conversation with Best-Selling
Author James Patterson." *Chicago Tribune.* June
9, 2014. Retrieved April 2015 (http://articles.
chicagotribune.com/2014-06-09/news/
ct-james-patterson-trice-met-0609-20140609_1_
james-patterson-trice-at-risk-kids).

Weinman, Sarah. "James Patterson Launches New
Children's Imprint." *Publisher's Marketplace*, May
29, 2015. Retrieved July 2015. (http://lunch.
publishersmarketplace.com/2015/05/
james-patterson-launches-new-childrens-
imprint/).

Wroe, Nicholas. "James Patterson: A Life in Writing."
Guardian, May 11, 2013. Retrieved April 2015
(http://www.theguardian.com/culture/2013/
may/11/james-patterson-life-in-writing).

Zaleski, Jeff. "The James Patterson Business."
Publishers Weekly, November 4, 2002. Retrieved
April 2015 (http://www.publishersweekly.com/pw/
print/20021104/21533-the-james-patterson-busi-
ness.html).

INDEX

ABOUT THE AUTHOR

Susan Nichols is an author and English teacher who lives in Baltimore, Maryland.

PHOTO CREDITS

Cover, pp. 3, 86 David Levenson/Getty Images; pp. 6-7 © Europa Newswire/Alamy; p. 11 © Philip Scalia/Alamy; pp. 14-15, 16-17, 58-59, 80 © ZUMA Press, Inc./Alamy; p. 21 Manhattan College Marketing & Communication; pp. 22-23 Stock Montage/Archive Photos/Getty Images; pp. 26-27 © Sean Pavone/Alamy; pp. 32-33, 39 © AF archive/Alamy; p. 36 Matthew Peyton/Getty Images; pp. 42-43, 46-47, 82-83 © AP Images; p. 51 Helga Esteb/Shutterstock.com; pp. 55, 62-63, 66-67 The Washington Post/Getty Images; p. 65 Robin Marchant/Getty Images; pp. 72-73 © 2014 NBA Entertainment. Photo by Gary Dineen/NBAE/Getty Images; p. 74 Twin Design/Shutterstock.com; pp. 76-77 Brent N. Clarke/FilmMagic/Getty Images; cover, interior pages (book) © www.istockphoto.com/Andrzej Tokarski, (textured background) javarman/Shutterstock.com; interior pages (moon over water) MidoSemsem/Shutterstock.com

Designer: Nicole Russo; Editor: Christine Poolos